Why things don't work
PLANE

www.raintreepublishers.co.uk
Visit our website to find out more information about
Raintree books.

To order:
☎ Phone 44 (0) 1865 888112
🖹 Send a fax to 44 (0) 1865 314091
💻 Visit the Raintree bookshop at
www.raintreepublishers.co.uk to browse our
catalogue and order online.

Why things don't work PLANE
was produced by

David West 🧍🧍 **Children's Books**
7 Princeton Court
55 Felsham Road
London SW15 1AZ

Editor: Dominique Crowley
Consultant: Nigel Parker

First published in Great Britain by
Raintree, Halley Court, Jordan Hill, Oxford OX2 8EJ, part of
Harcourt Education. Raintree is a registered trademark of Harcourt
Education Ltd.

10 digit ISBN: 1 4062 0545 1
13 digit ISBN: 978 1 4062 0545 9

11 10 09 08 07
10 9 8 7 6 5 4 3 2 1

British Library Cataloguing in Publication Data

West, David
    Plane. - (Why things don't work)
    1.Airplanes - Maintenance and repair - Comic books,
    strips,
    etc. - Juvenile literature
    I.Title
    629.1'346

Printed and bound in China

Why things don't work

PLANE

by David West

Raintree

Contents

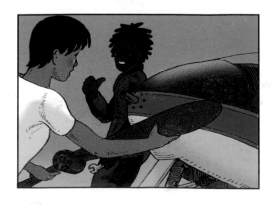

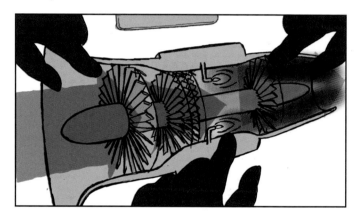

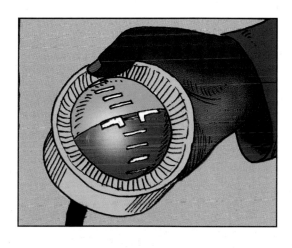

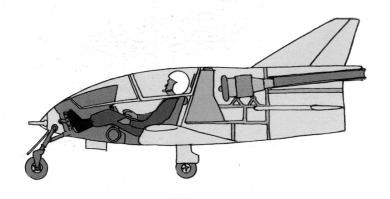

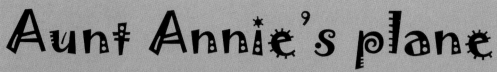

Aunt Annie's plane

ALICE HAS JUST PASSED HER FLYING TEST AND WANTS TO FLY HER AUNT'S PLANE. UNFORTUNATELY, IT DOESN'T WORK. IT HASN'T BEEN FLOWN FOR YEARS AND THERE ARE PARTS OF THE PLANE SCATTERED ABOUT.

ALSO, THERE SEEM TO BE A FEW OTHER PROBLEMS...

THE PISTON ENGINE IS MISSING.

SOME INSTRUMENTS ARE MISSING FROM THE INSTRUMENT PANEL.

THE LANDING GEAR IS FAULTY.

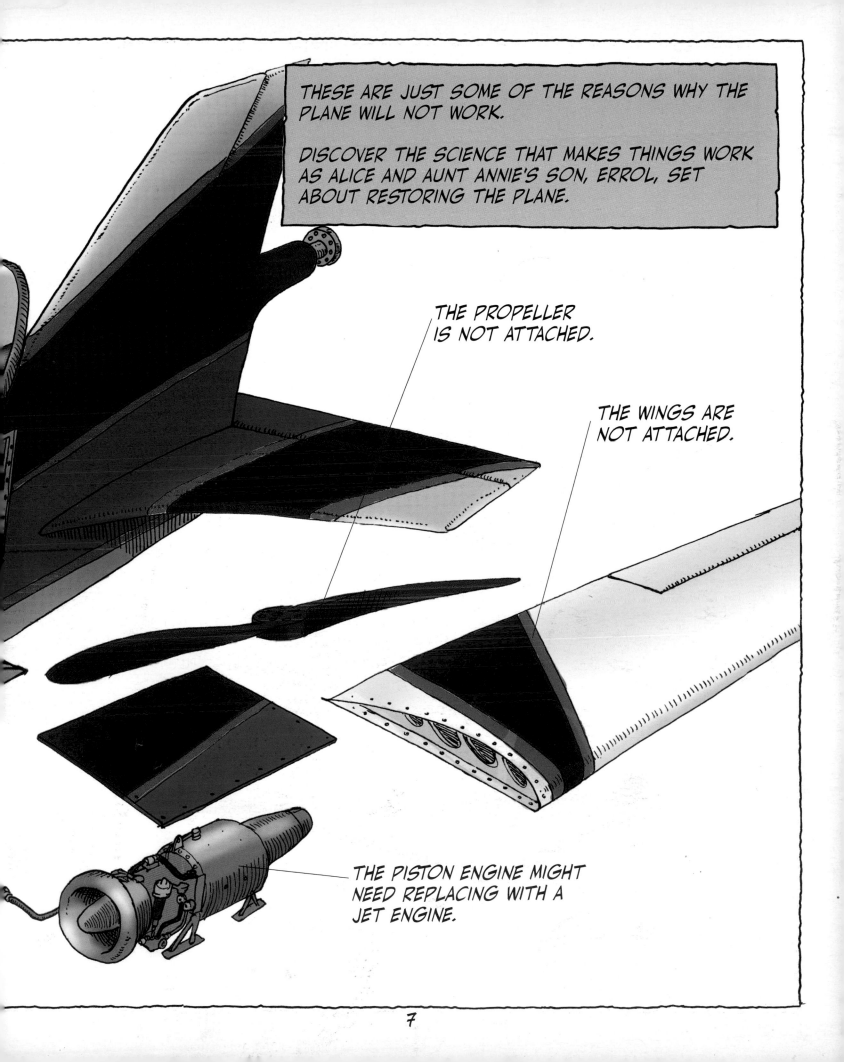

THESE ARE JUST SOME OF THE REASONS WHY THE PLANE WILL NOT WORK.

DISCOVER THE SCIENCE THAT MAKES THINGS WORK AS ALICE AND AUNT ANNIE'S SON, ERROL, SET ABOUT RESTORING THE PLANE.

THE PROPELLER IS NOT ATTACHED.

THE WINGS ARE NOT ATTACHED.

THE PISTON ENGINE MIGHT NEED REPLACING WITH A JET ENGINE.

IT'S HARD KNOWING WHERE TO START.

LET'S START WITH THE ENGINE.

IT'S A PISTON ENGINE, ISN'T IT?

YES, IT'S THE TYPE OF ENGINE YOU GET IN CARS. I'LL SHOW YOU.

INSIDE, THERE ARE FOUR PISTONS.

SIDE VIEW

Four pistons

FRONT VIEW

Fuel and air

Combustion chamber

IN EACH PISTON, AIR AND FUEL ARE SUCKED INTO THE COMBUSTION CHAMBER AND THEN SQUEEZED INTO A SMALL SPACE.

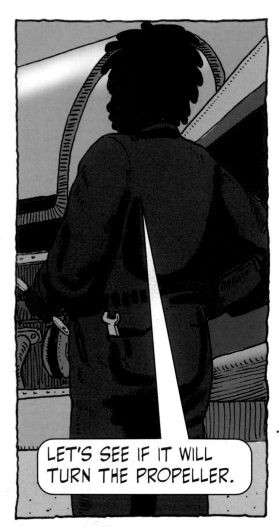

THE BLADES ON A PROPELLER ARE SHAPED LIKE THIS.

WHEN THEY SPIN, THE AIR RUSHING OVER THE FRONT SURFACE HAS FURTHER TO TRAVEL. THIS CREATES A **LOW AIR PRESSURE** AREA IN FRONT.

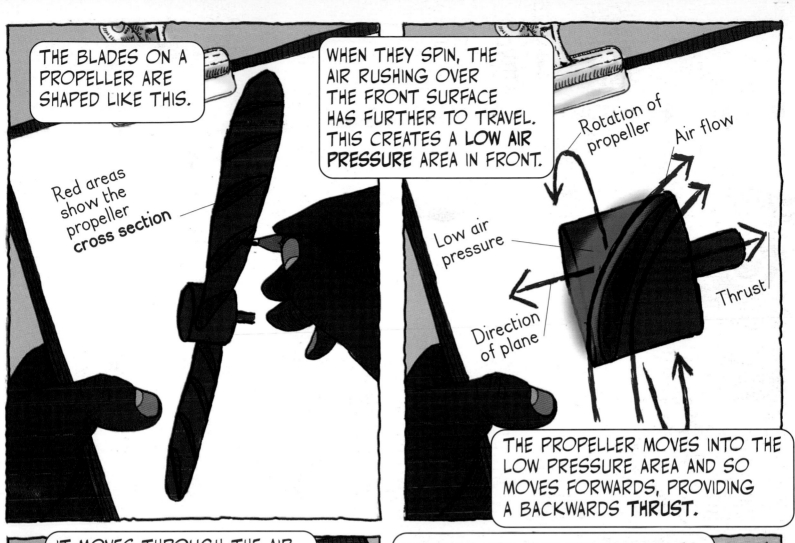

Red areas show the propeller **cross section**

Rotation of propeller

Air flow

Low air pressure

Direction of plane

Thrust

THE PROPELLER MOVES INTO THE LOW PRESSURE AREA AND SO MOVES FORWARDS, PROVIDING A BACKWARDS **THRUST**.

IT MOVES THROUGH THE AIR LIKE A SCREW. THIS IS WHY PROPELLERS ARE SOMETIMES CALLED AIRSCREWS.

WHETHER YOU PUT THE PROPELLER AT THE FRONT OR AT THE BACK IT STILL MOVES THE PLANE IN THE SAME DIRECTION.

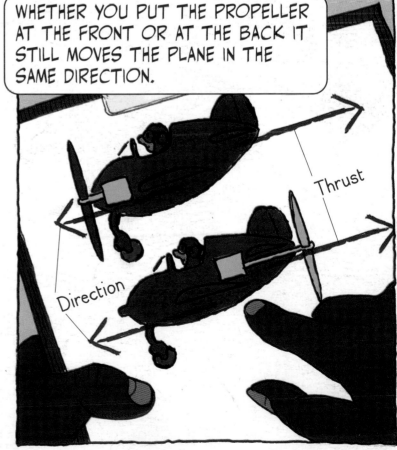

Thrust

Direction

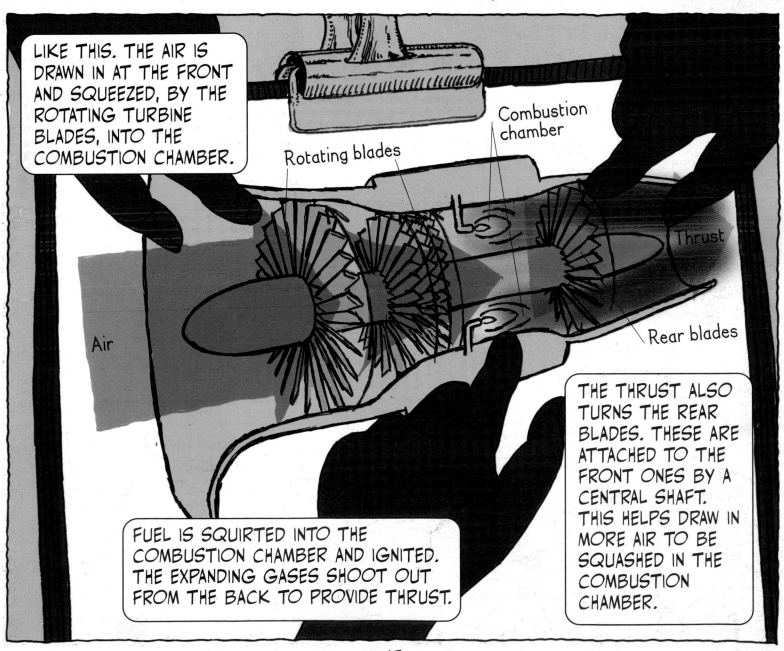

CAN IT TURN A PROPELLER?

NO NEED. IT PROVIDES ITS OWN THRUST.

HOW DOES IT DO THAT?

LIKE THIS. THE AIR IS DRAWN IN AT THE FRONT AND SQUEEZED, BY THE ROTATING TURBINE BLADES, INTO THE COMBUSTION CHAMBER.

Combustion chamber

Rotating blades

Thrust

Air

Rear blades

FUEL IS SQUIRTED INTO THE COMBUSTION CHAMBER AND IGNITED. THE EXPANDING GASES SHOOT OUT FROM THE BACK TO PROVIDE THRUST.

THE THRUST ALSO TURNS THE REAR BLADES. THESE ARE ATTACHED TO THE FRONT ONES BY A CENTRAL SHAFT. THIS HELPS DRAW IN MORE AIR TO BE SQUASHED IN THE COMBUSTION CHAMBER.

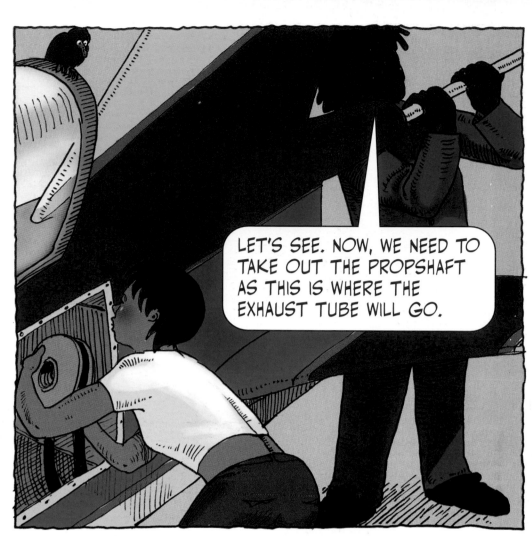

SOON, WE HAD THE JET ENGINE FITTED.

JET ENGINES USE A DIFFERENT FUEL FROM PISTON ENGINES. SO WE HAD BETTER CHANGE THE FUEL.

LET'S SEE IF THE ENGINE WORKS.

WEEEEEEEEEEEE

NICE.

LIFT

18

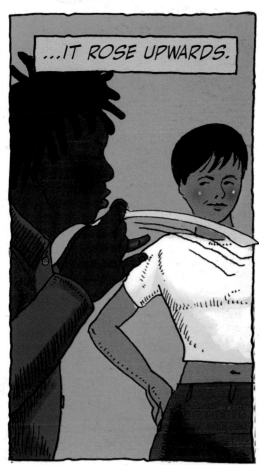

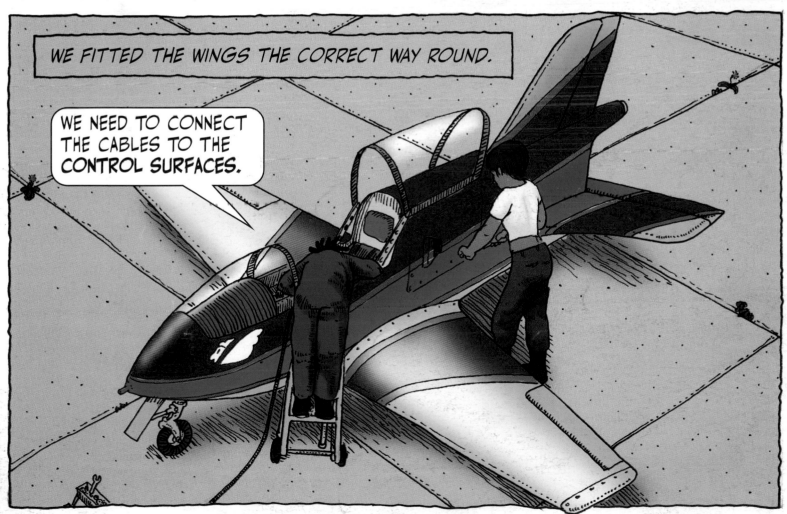

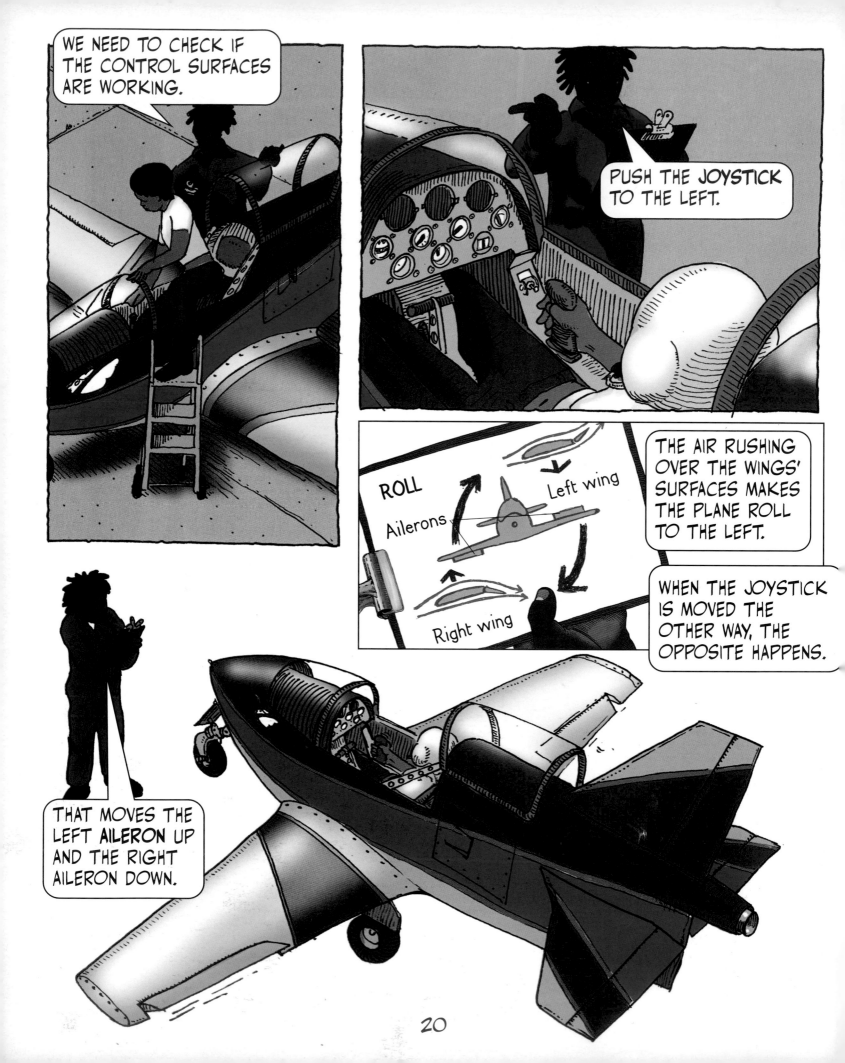

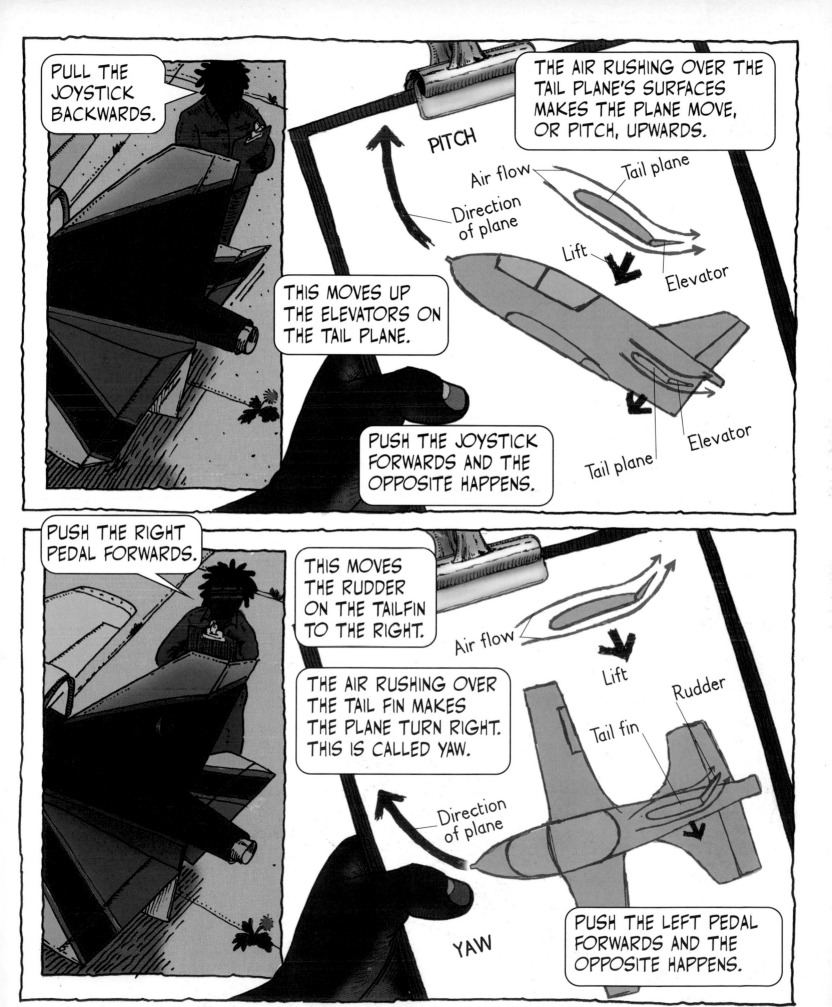

WHILE YOU ARE IN THE COCKPIT, WE MIGHT AS WELL CHECK THE INSTRUMENT PANEL.

THERE ARE SOME MISSING.

IT'S OK. I HAVE THEM HERE.

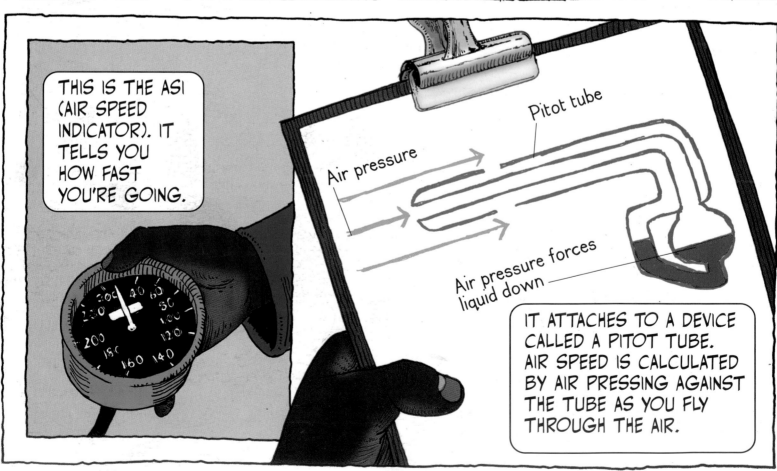

THIS IS THE ASI (AIR SPEED INDICATOR). IT TELLS YOU HOW FAST YOU'RE GOING.

Pitot tube

Air pressure

Air pressure forces liquid down

IT ATTACHES TO A DEVICE CALLED A PITOT TUBE. AIR SPEED IS CALCULATED BY AIR PRESSING AGAINST THE TUBE AS YOU FLY THROUGH THE AIR.

THIS IS THE ALTIMETER. IT TELLS YOU HOW HIGH YOU ARE FLYING.

THIS WORKS BY MEASURING **AIR PRESSURE**, WHICH CHANGES AT DIFFERENT HEIGHTS.

Air pressure is weaker the higher you go, so the balloon gets bigger

Air pressure at sea level keeps the balloon small

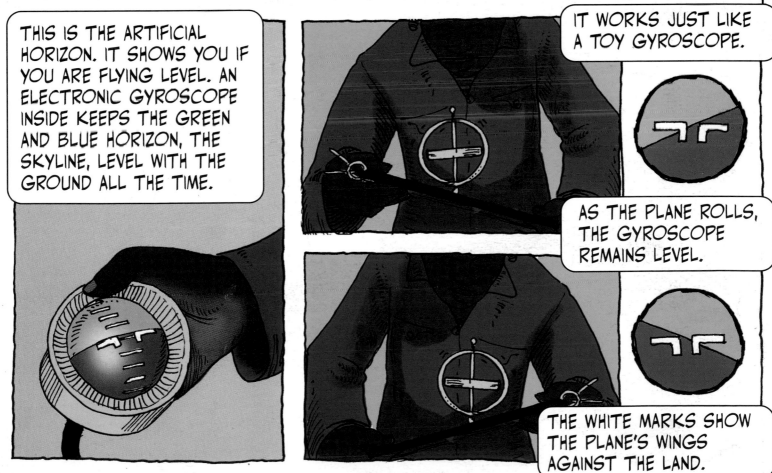

THIS IS THE ARTIFICIAL HORIZON. IT SHOWS YOU IF YOU ARE FLYING LEVEL. AN ELECTRONIC GYROSCOPE INSIDE KEEPS THE GREEN AND BLUE HORIZON, THE SKYLINE, LEVEL WITH THE GROUND ALL THE TIME.

IT WORKS JUST LIKE A TOY GYROSCOPE.

AS THE PLANE ROLLS, THE GYROSCOPE REMAINS LEVEL.

THE WHITE MARKS SHOW THE PLANE'S WINGS AGAINST THE LAND.

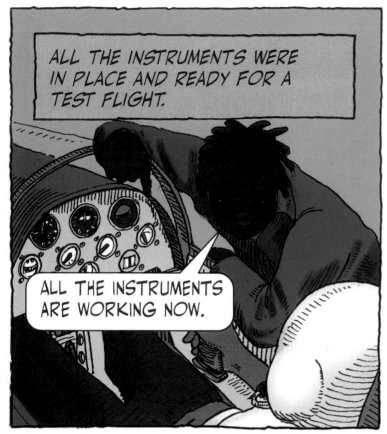

ALL THE INSTRUMENTS WERE IN PLACE AND READY FOR A TEST FLIGHT.

ALL THE INSTRUMENTS ARE WORKING NOW.

ERROL WENT INTO THE CONTROL TOWER TO CHECK FOR OTHER AIR TRAFFIC.

ALICE, YOU CAN TAXI OUT TO THE RUNWAY.

ROGER THAT, ERROL.

YOU ARE CLEAR FOR TAKE OFF.

ROGER THAT, ERROL.

WHOOOOOOOSH

24

26

THE FOLLOWING WEEK, WE SET OFF FOR AN AIR SHOW.

WE SAW A COPY OF THE WRIGHT FLYER.

THIS WAS THE FIRST PLANE TO FLY. IT WAS MADE AND FLOWN BY THE WRIGHT BROTHERS IN 1904.

THERE WERE ALSO SOME AMAZING PLANES FROM THE SECOND WORLD WAR.

LOOK IT'S A FLYING FORTRESS BOMBER.

AND A MUSTANG FIGHTER.

THEN, SOME AWESOME STEALTH FIGHTERS FLEW BY.

WE ALSO SAW THE WORLD'S BIGGEST MODEL AIRCRAFT.

IT'S AN AIRBUS SUPERJUMBO. THE JET ENGINES ARE REAL MINIATURE JET ENGINES!

THEN IT WAS MY TURN...

...AND HERE COMES ALICE IN A BD-5, THE THE WORLD'S SMALLEST JET PLANE.

Parts of a plane

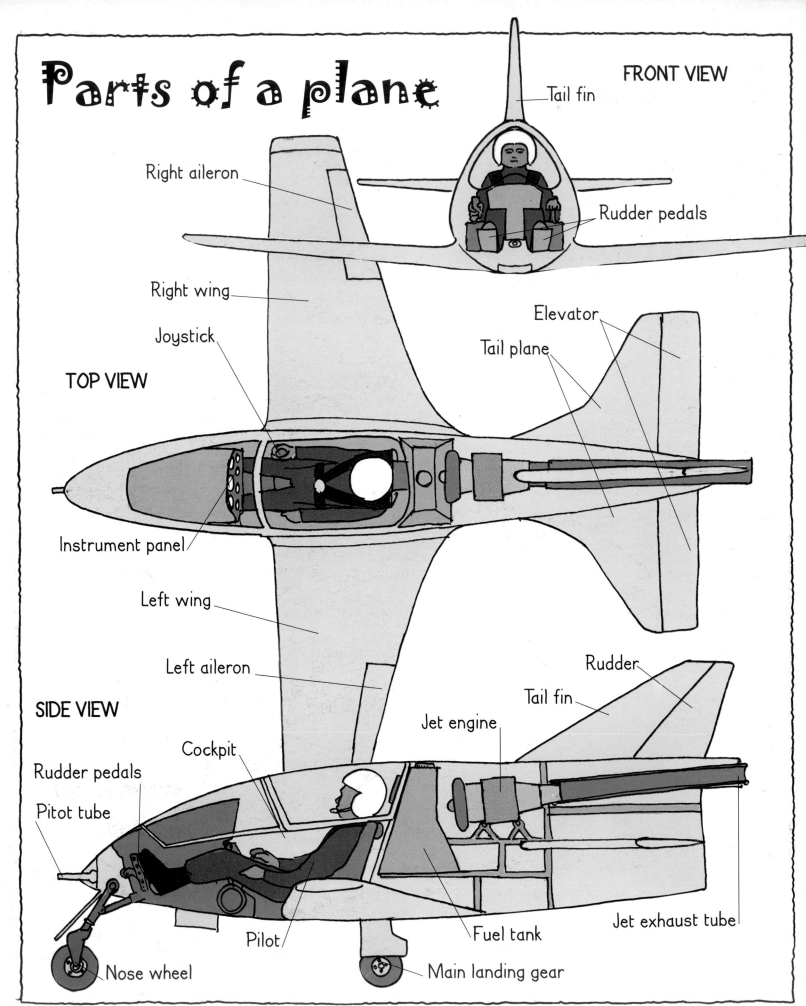

FRONT VIEW

Tail fin

Right aileron

Rudder pedals

Right wing

Elevator

Joystick

Tail plane

TOP VIEW

Instrument panel

Left wing

Left aileron

Rudder

SIDE VIEW

Tail fin

Jet engine

Cockpit

Rudder pedals

Pitot tube

Pilot

Fuel tank

Jet exhaust tube

Nose wheel

Main landing gear

Glossary

AILERONS
MOVABLE FLAPS ON THE WINGS THAT
MAKE THE PLANE ROLL

AIR PRESSURE
THE FORCE OF AIR CREATED BY THE
AMOUNT, OR MOVEMENT OF AIR

COMBUSTION CHAMBER
THE AREA OF AN ENGINE WHERE THE
FUEL/AIR MIXTURE IS SET ALIGHT

CONTROL SURFACES
THE MOVABLE PARTS ON THE WINGS AND
TAIL OF A PLANE THAT CONTROL THE WAY
THE PLANE MOVES IN THE AIR

CRANKSHAFT
THE ROTATING SHAFT AT THE BOTTOM
OF THE ENGINE THAT IS TURNED BY
THE PISTONS

CROSS SECTION
THE SHAPE OF AN OBJECT WHEN IT IS
SLICED THROUGH BY AN IMAGINARY BLADE

ELEVATORS
MOVABLE FLAPS ON THE TAIL PLANE THAT
MAKE THE PLANE PITCH UP OR DOWN

HYDRAULIC FLUID
SPECIAL LIQUID USED TO MOVE PISTONS

IGNITE
TO SET ALIGHT

JOYSTICK
THE HAND-OPERATED CONTROL COLUMN
THAT CONTROLS THE ROLL AND PITCH OF
THE PLANE

LANDING GEAR
WHEELS AND SUPPORTING PARTS OF
A PLANE THAT ALLOW IT TO TAKE OFF
AND LAND

LOW AIR PRESSURE AREA
AN AREA OF AIR THAT HAS LESS AIR THAN
ITS SURROUNDING AREA. IF THE PRESSURE
IS LOW ENOUGH IT WILL DRAW IN OBJECTS
OR AIR TO EQUALISE THE PRESSURE.

PISTON
A METAL CYLINDER THAT MOVES TO AND
FRO INSIDE ANOTHER CYLINDER

PROPSHAFT (PROPELLER SHAFT)
A REVOLVING ROD THAT CONNECTS THE
ENGINE TO THE PROPELLER

RUDDER
MOVABLE FLAP ON THE TAIL FIN THAT
MAKES THE PLANE YAW LEFT OR RIGHT

SPARK PLUG
A DEVICE THAT, WHEN AN ELECTRICAL
CURRENT IS PASSED THROUGH IT, CAUSES
A SPARK TO BE CREATED

THRUST
A STRONG CONTINUOUS FORCE OF
PRESSURE

Index

See how they grow

Dogs

Kathryn Walker

WAYLAND

First published in 2007
by Wayland

Copyright © Wayland 2007

Wayland
338 Euston Road
London NW1 3BH

Wayland Australia
Hachette Children's Books
Level 17/207 Kent Street
Sydney, NSW 2000

British Library Cataloguing in Publication Data
Walker, Kathryn, 1957-
    Dog. - (See how they grow)
    1. Dogs - Juvenile literature
    2. Puppies - Juvenile literature
    I. Title
    636.7'07

ISBN-13: 9780750252539

Printed in China
Wayland is a division of Hachette Children's Books,
an Hachette Livre UK company.

The publishers would like to thank the following
for allowing us to reproduce their pictures in
this book:
Corbis: title page and 14 (Chris Collins), 7 (Tim
Davis), 8 (Stapleton Collection), 9 (Ariel Skelley),
12 (Jim Craigmyle), 17 (Dewitt Jones).
Discovery Picture Library: 23. FLPA: cover
and 18 (Mark Raycroft/Minden Pictures), 5
(Angela Hampton), 13 (Foto Natura Stock).
Getty Images: 6 (Andy Rouse/Image Bank), 10
(Joseph H Bailey/National Geographic),
15 (GKHart/Vikki Hart/Photographer's Choice),
19 (Richard Schultz/Taxi), 21 (Denis Felix).
Istockphoto: 4 (Sonyae), 11 (Danielle Danford),
16 (Iztok Noc), 20 (Willie B. Thomas), 22
(Anne Clark).

Contents

What is a dog?

People in many countries like to keep pet dogs. Pet dogs are known as **domestic dogs**. They belong to a family of animals called the **canids**. Wolves, foxes and wild dogs are all members of this family.

▼ A pet dog can become an important part of the family.

Dogs have very good hearing. They also have a powerful sense of smell. Dogs can smell things that people cannot smell.

▲ Dogs sniff each other when they meet. This is how they get to know one another.

Dog Fact

Some types of dogs have a better sense of smell than others. These include bloodhounds and beagles.

Wild dogs

There are wild dogs in most parts of the world. Wolves and some wild dogs live and **hunt** in groups. These groups are called **packs**.

▼ African wild dogs live in the grasslands of Africa.

Dog Fact

About 15,000 years ago, some wolves began living with people. All pet dogs have come from these **tame** wolves.

▲ All pet dogs are related to the grey wolf, or timber wolf.

Domestic dogs

Dogs were the first animals to be kept by people. Dogs were very useful. They helped people to hunt. Dogs also made good guards and companions.

Dog Fact

There are about 600 million domestic dogs in the world.

◀ The ancient Egyptians kept dogs for hunting and as pets. This picture shows an Egyptian hunting scene.

Dogs that are well looked after can make wonderful pets. They will form strong bonds with their owners. Dogs can be very loving and playful.

▲ Dogs like to live in packs. To a pet dog, its owners are its pack.

A puppy is born

A young dog is called a **puppy**. A small mother dog can have up to six puppies in a **litter**. Bigger dogs can have as many as twelve. When they are born, the puppies are blind and deaf.

▼ For the first few weeks, puppies feed on their mother's milk.

A puppy's ears and eyes open when it is about two weeks old. By three weeks it can walk and **bark**. It can even wag its tail.

▲ Young puppies huddle together to keep warm.

Growing up

A puppy starts growing teeth when it is four weeks old. Now it can start to eat solid food. At eight weeks old, a puppy is ready to leave its mother.

▼ Young puppies need four or five small meals a day.

Dogs usually live for between twelve and fourteen years. Some types of dog have shorter lives. Others may live up to twenty years. Small dogs often live longer than large dogs.

▲ As they get old, dogs sleep more and eat less.

Dog Fact

A female dog is able to have puppies when she is six months old.

All sorts of dogs

There are many different types of dog. Special types of dog are called **breeds**. There are hundreds of different breeds. Many dogs are a mix of breeds.

One of the tallest dogs is the Irish Wolfhound. It can grow to be more than 90 cm tall. The Chihuahua is one of the smallest breeds.

▼ There are many different breeds of dog. They come in all shapes and sizes.

This Great Dane towers over a Jack Russell terrier.

15

How dogs can help us

Some dogs are trained as guide dogs. They help blind people to get about. Police use specially trained dogs, too. They use sniffer dogs to sniff out drugs or **explosives**. They sometimes use tracker dogs to help them find people.

▼ Husky dogs are used to pull sleds through snow.

▼ This sheepdog is helping the farmer to herd and guard his sheep.

17

Choosing a pet dog

Only get a pet dog if you are sure you can give it lots of time and care. Then you can choose whether to have a puppy or an older dog. Rescue shelters have lots of dogs needing homes.

▼ These German Shepherd puppies will grow up to be large dogs. They will need lots of space and exercise.

Some people like **pedigree** dogs. These are dogs whose parents are of the same breed. Others prefer to have dogs that do not belong to any one breed.

▲ This dog is a mix of different breeds. Dogs like this are known as **mongrels**.

Caring for a dog

Your new pet will need to visit the vet for **vaccinations**. These are injections that will protect a dog against some serious diseases.

◀ All dogs should see a vet for a health check once a year.

Dogs need at least two meals a day and water to drink to stay healthy. Dried or tinned dog food gives them the goodness they need. Bones or chews will help keep their teeth strong.

▲ Dogs need to be brushed regularly. Sometimes they need to have baths.

Outdoor life

It is important to train your dog to behave well. You can do this by rewarding the dog when it does something right. Never hit or shout at your dog.

You will need to walk your dog at least twice a day. The exercise will help keep it fit, healthy and happy.

Some people take their pets to dog training classes.

▼ Your dog will love to play outdoor games with you.

Glossary

bark
A loud cry made by a dog.

breed
A special type of dog.

canids
Family of animals that includes dogs, wolves, foxes and jackals.

domestic dog
A dog that lives with people and is kept as a pet.

explosives
A substance or device that causes an explosion.

hunt
To chase and kill an animal for food.

litter
The offspring, or young, born to an animal at one time.

mongrel
A dog that does not belong to one breed.

pack
A group of animals, such as dogs, that live and hunt together.

pedigree
A type of dog whose parents were both of the same breed

puppy
A young dog.

tame
A wild animal that has become used to people.

vaccination
An injection that is given to protect people or animals against some serious diseases.

Index